disappeared

Also by Jasmine V. Bailey

Alexandria

disappeared

jasmine v. bailey

Carnegie Mellon University Press
Pittsburgh 2017

Acknowledgments

The author gratefully acknowledges the publications in which versions of these poems first appeared:

94 Creations: "Elegy with Africa," "Medea"
Big River Poetry Review: "Sourdough"
Cimarron Review: "The Lover," "Flowers Are Not Women," "Fractal Geometry"
Crab Orchard Review: "The Heaven of Poets"
DoveTales Literary Journal: "Elegy with the Soviet Union," "Elegy with Argentina," "Elegy with Nicaragua"
Duende: "Siddhartha," "Disappeared"
Ghost City Review: "Apologia for Lechers," "Love in the Emergency Room"
Inch: "Portrait of a Young Man"
Lilliput: "Perhaps"
Nine Mile Magazine: "Theory of Relativity," "Mentor," "Palimpsest," "Equity," "Garden"
Poet Lore: "To the Departing Beloved"
Quarterly West: "Scheherazade," "The Working Class"
Slipstream: "Palimpsest"
Slushpile: "Katabasis"
South Carolina Review: "Fuji"
The Carolina Quarterly: "Kingfisher"
The Midwest Quarterly: "Every Day You Are the Oldest You've Ever Been"
the minnesota review: "Full Moon"
The Potomac/A Journal of Poetry and Politics: "Love Poem for Malcolm X"
Valparaiso Poetry Review: "Procession of Santa Lucia"

"Diamonds on the Soles of Her Shoes" appeared in *12 Women: an anthology of poems* published by Carnegie Mellon University Press in 2014.

"Perhaps" and "Katabasis" appeared in the chapbook *Sleep and What Precedes It*, winner of the 2009 Longleaf Press Chapbook prize.

Book design by Shaune Marx & Connie Amoroso

Contents

Part I

Palimpsest | 9
Garden | 10
Lenox | 11
Equity | 12
The Working Class | 14
Sourdough | 15
Elegy with Nicaragua | 16
Eventually the Ocean | 17
Love in the Emergency Room | 18
Scheherazade | 20
First Day of School | 21
Diamonds on the Soles of Her Shoes | 22
Full Moon | 24
Apologia for Lechers | 25

Part II

Elegy with Argentina | 29
Mentor | 30
Grave | 31
Stay of Execution | 32
Biography of a Poet | 34
Portrait of a Young Man | 35
Palimpsest | 36
Perhaps | 37
Feast of the Assumption | 38
Medea | 40
Disappeared | 41
Videla in Prison | 42
A Story about Departure | 43
Siddhartha | 44
Theory of Relativity | 45

Part III

Fractal Geometry | 49
Flowers Are Not Women | 51
The Lover | 52
Survivor | 53
The Heaven of Poets | 54
Elegy with Africa | 56
Phaeton | 58
Love Poem for Malcolm X | 59
To the Departing Beloved | 61
Procession of Santa Lucia | 63
Fuji | 64
Katabasis | 65
You Are in Ukraine | 66
Elegy with the Soviet Union | 67
Kingfisher | 68
Every Day You Are the Oldest You've Ever Been | 70

Part I

Truly, though our element is time,
We are not suited to the long perspectives
Open at each instant of our lives.
They link us to our losses: worse,
They show us what we have as it once was,
Blindingly undiminished, just as though
By acting differently, we could have kept it so.

—Philip Larkin

Palimpsest

By night an angel floats down Egg Harbor's yellow streets,
or a Victorian ghost, or a cripple on a three-wheel bike
who everyone knows but whose name no one knows.
He sings, his white cardigan open in the soft draft.
On the pike, a shack advertises "B&D fetish," lit
for the first time you know of, two ghosts' cars parked
at opposite ends of its little lot. The abandoned Acme
where your brother discovered a boy hanging
looks more natural in the dim streetlamp the town
has overlooked removing. On the sidewalk, spots of blood
or scraps of shell, the lingering smell of bad crab
people grew used to and stopped taking back.

Noel Pinkus's house is no worse than when he lived,
though his many bikes go unsanded. From his crowded porch
it's just a few blocks up Hamburg to the cemetery
where people only mothers remember are buried
and certainly do not lay at rest. They mottle the humidity
with mother-of-pearl faces of another century,
sensibility, a sadness the light of the day blots,
its definition gone from dictionaries. Join them stroking
the bluebird houses, grazing the candy-red geraniums.
Step carefully over the plots, as you did as a child, unsure
where to put your foot; squint for your fading name.

Garden

In the glass shards and clamshells,
the deep, dense root that felt like a chest
against the spade, or the wilted box cradling
a dog, Styrofoam with most of the word *McNugget*,
the yard teemed with evidence of regret.

The attic divided along the orderly and decaying;
there had been time to think before stuffing pictures
into a wicker lunchbox, a half-hearted plan to return
to the silver dress from 1966, the marionette
in torn plastic melted and frozen over and over.

Some things are forgotten naturally, blotted
by the inward-casting sheen of living in oneself.
More is lost on purpose: ceremony of burial,
sacrament of beating with a shovel, sowing
a concealing patch of mint.

Sift the dirt for radishes and behold the miracle
of how few people are hidden beneath the grass.
Denser than lead beneath their cairn, pressurized
by intent. The land is inky with torn pages
from the comedy of getting the better of the past.

Lenox

At birth no one guaranteed your meals
or a quiet place to study, but like anyone
you were welcome to sweat for china
until you could be trusted with gold paint.
The secretary, mad with power over the intercom,
played Brenda Lee until you quit
to get a job at Mac's serving oysters to men
who insulted and propositioned you until you quit
when you had the money to apply to college.

It used to be American to be poor and learn to read
and die in Vietnam with Faulkner in your pocket.
You smoked hashish and ate potato chips,
attempted astral projection from the floor
that held your first Thanksgiving cole slaw,
a baby's crib and a pallet of kittens.
In all those years you never had a job,
no matter how you examined it,
that led to anyone dying. That used to be
what they called a good life.

Equity

I know we will have it, a house
that belongs to us by contract,
bought with capital, recognized by courts.
What is it we've been doing in all these apartments
owned by tall men with teams of women
doing their screaming for them? The dream
must have been on hold, but sometimes
I failed to remember that was so.

I know we shall have some earth
surveyed, rendered mathematic,
owned as I have owned sandwiches
and some shoes: without dispute. Ours
to do with. To set a couch on the porch
or to stud with iridescent balls on columns.
To landscape with drought-resistant
succulents and wild thyme.
To come out with a golf club and scream
Get the fuck off my lawn,
to die in or away from.

How much will we believe it's ours?
The vast, timeless hawthorn one of us will climb
after an argument over money
whose branches our daughter will dance with
calling them prince this, prince that.
The spot that is always a little damp below the floodplain
good for digging worms,
the border where we bury animal after animal
and erect pagan remembrances of stones
and walnut shells.

Day after day you hand me coffee
and it is no accident that your fingers
look like tributaries of the Amazon
or the branches coming off of a wild cherry.
The fact of pattern is proof

of all patterns. I let it serve as evidence
of something as impossible as separating
coffee back to water and beans.
Take my hand like the Orinoco and promise
that soon we will build our next lie.

The Working Class

The world works its hands between you and I
as it runs its fingers over faces
leaving a map of its pleasure
and corn records the anger of a man
who chases deer in his truck
because of a woman. The plows answer
faithfully the vespers, averring early morning
when a wife is awake discovering misfortune
and not praying for something else.
It feels like someone wants us to grow
apart, but actually no one thinks of us.

If a reprieve loses its way here, we will toss it
into the well with the wine and soup.
We would not know what to do
with the things we longed for.
We listen to the hurt and hungry,
dissolve our hands in dishwater,
sweep up the dust after it settles
after we sweep it up. A magazine reveals
that it is made of us.

Sourdough

She made a present of her body
to the loaf, moisture in the skin and spit
and tip of tongue, pressure in the palm,
heat from the bands of muscles in the arm
and vessels that open in the hands like leaves.

Her feet braced the ocean of the knead,
knees absorbed the tide, fatigue,
and locked the torso to its commitment:
heave the chest and shoulders where the blood
was doing its unthinking, impermanent
work—striking time steady as a leaking sink,
softer than a redwing babbles its affairs.

That the body can crush from either end
towards its center without collapse is what
bread means, and is not a miracle.
Neither that yeast lives invisible in air
or under fingernails. A quotidian affair,
like raking leaves or checking into a hospital.

It was enough without the thrill or fuss
of grace, even with the sacrifice
to sandwiches and mold.

Elegy with Nicaragua

I was forever spilling watermelon juice, stretching
uselessly in the millennial heat. Dust remade us—
we forgot whether we had showered in the trickle
that never wet our scalps or were cleaned by jocote
or the Pacific or one another's tongues—lousy
with mangoes and uncultivated flowers, sewing thread
just holding our clothes together, Alemán just holding
the country together, the blood in the streets old enough
to drink a beer in the United States, unlike us.

•

We drove an oven to the sweltering San Juan
and the studio where everything—windows, floor,
the men working—were made of clay, turning pots
on kick wheels, cutting gods out of the sides,
feather-skirt, firebird, ordering the inexhaustible mess
and shipping it to Manhattan. At the shanty city
bordering the landfill, everyone was poorer than you,
your house wood and a sheaf of tin. Your body, too,
a miracle of economy, so thin you might think
the soul would be easier to find, and it was.

•

The *tinaja* and the fanged bird say *Nicaragua*
to anyone who will listen; we move like sugar in tea,
kites tangling and loosening. It was possible once
for a few córdobas to buy a bag of jocotes,
sit at a footrace and try to figure out how to eat them,
the mess of flesh and skin and seeds, or not eat them,
but taste in them the tongue of someone
you just now realize you love, the dwindling jungle,
the clumsy, indifferent ocean, the soiled lakes, the sweetness—
I don't know if you still eat them, but you remember.

Eventually the Ocean

Aging loss and diurnal love,
colonizing as moss,
as a clonal species that looks like a forest

but is really one tree.
They do not resemble the tempest
of the young, strong girl I was.

They look like almost nothing,
as the Atlantic is a dun line
in sun and dead calm.

I stop with full hands
mourning what made each shell.
Eventually the ocean

will sweep us out like a reed whose roots
have loosened from the dunes.

The vows we make in some blind of immortality
stitch my wrists painfully
to the silk earth,

where I imagine a tremor
gathering in the restless plates,
and am right.

Love in the Emergency Room

Homeless fall here as often as they are able
to sleep in the heart-starting fluorescent light,
still as a urine cup.
Dan leans against the cot where I scream
and grow brave on Percocet.
He is normal except for the ways
in which he is exceptional;
this makes him truly normal.
He wears the suit in which he married me,
given to him by a friend moving to Russia.
The night he left we drank PBR in the only dive
in Cambridge, Massachusetts.

I try to make St. Lucians tell me about home,
to remember some of "Omeros."
But every day feels this way:
people walk blindly wearing cares
on their bodies like skin. Some have fallen in a heap.
Some take pity and tell me a story.
They like that I require little;
it's easier to be good. It's never long
before they reveal something
that troubles them. They don't know what to do
with the homeless who want turkey sandwiches,
to say nothing of their daughters.
I want to love the heap which seems dead
but is a person.
I should lift him in my arms and teach him
how to change everything: personal hygiene,
college matriculation, but my arm is broken
and I have started screaming again
from the merest shift. I see now

that no one really has the use of their arms.
No one needs only one turkey sandwich.
Dan is normal, but sometimes
his talent makes him seem invulnerable.

I like that. Everybody likes that.
My fingers sag. Even the air
is more than I can lift. My soul
is not as limitless as the color green
in a forest renewed by rain.
My body feels
more shatterable in this polyester dress
meant to look like a Grecian robe but which
is clearly some factory-made shit from Macy's.
My wisdom is like a coin in an inner pocket
that could not buy a candy bar at a bus stop.

The face of the man who gave Dan his suit
is soft, sad, and sweet like Georgian wine.
He gained too much weight to wear the suit
but the weight made him beautiful.
He has a noise that means: sad and funny.
He gets better the later it is, the more we've drunk.
For him the world should be nocturnal
and less ignorant. Young,
I failed to see that to be extraordinary
is a gift granted to everyone who is loved.
I didn't know that what was rare and valuable
was the way one leans into the cot,
not heroic, not collapsing.
The bagel with cream cheese, the steady gait,
the one you love because he's yours,
like a plot of land, like the moment you are born
to your weird parents
to the one in which your heart
finally gets over blood.

Scheherazade

We can no longer call this summer August.
Two bats dart from mosquito to mosquito
and the half-coin moon is a hieroglyph for work.
From the soy field something wild and alone cries.
We touch everything briefly,
but the fact of touch lasts unpityingly.
I drove down the road, seeing my little house
for the first, then the second time, someday
to move out. Runner after runner goes by toward
where the turnpike bursts like a bad epiphany
from the tricycle-strewn town. The deafening crickets
never finish their shifting story.

First Day of School

The sloping path is new and bright for the frightened, tight,
exhilarated people that circle you. Their unmade oaths and betrayals,
unwritten masques, electrify the stinging air.

Can you lay the loss of fall at your husband's feet?
If he fails to see you as a phoenix, as an apocalypse,
or to see that like Prometheus and no one else you have a flint,

and it is this special access to fire he lives on?
Yes, he has taken from you the meaning of leaves and air.
He has entailed your birthlands to the drunken peasants

who misunderstand even religion.
He refuses you the ocean and its octopi, its tragedies of halibut fishing,
and of halibut, curtaining the sea's piebald floor.

How to fight when the bravery to die is needed,
and those who have it are drunk on Monday,
and Monday gives itself to them

like the sweet-hearted virgin you never were or even met.
Perhaps it is you who sent the last of the china to the moneylender
and lost her address, so that you have to eat from shoes.

You, certainly, who catered some funeral of vegetarians,
throwing cleavers into your pocketbook. Your madness, stagnant and colicky,
threatens to rend fall apart at the seam—

close it comes to trying when he arrives in a soiled tie waving his arms.
He is fresh, like before he knew you, full of noble outrage,
and you live on him.

Diamonds on the Soles of Her Shoes

We ended up by sleeping in a doorway.

—Paul Simon

They were more ironic when we weren't in Williamsburg
or anywhere in Brooklyn, when for a decent slice of pizza
we might as well go to Naples, and the one Orthodox Jew

padded everywhere Saturdays chewing lavender pastries,
blessing the people in line for that week's two
forbidden films. You could see the impressions they left

alongside Amish hoofprints and trace her direction
if you could follow the smell of voile. All the town's diamonds
came from elsewhere, not just the DRC—an Armenian jeweler

in Hoboken, an unloved aunt who died, a blustery proposal
aboard a cruise the widow's too dotty to remember.
She didn't have to put her feet up for you to recognize them:

every strand of hair, the useless belt, light filtering
through Chinatown sunglasses, proved them: she just didn't need
what anybody had. Not the out-of-print book machine

or worried-over coffee of Soho, not the Bolshoi or Seine. They wore
like an Italian blazer from the eighties or a Kayan neck ring.
She tied a nylon around her cell phone and dragged it, crooning

Mapuche, saying, *It's me or it.* We colonized a swingset,
a gravestone, a stranded worm, broke into the First Madison Baptist Church,
the public library, the Korean nail shop, the Upstate Yoga Institute.

We demanded karaoke and refused to sing out loud, ordered Dubonnet
and threw the Drambuie they brought us at a cop. We made
off on someone's bike, getting a flat at the Elks Lodge where old men

smeared us with advice. She was a twenty-year-old man,
she was toothy, she was finite and hilarious. Steadily everything
became true, tinted green and yellow and see-through, then

evaporated in the morning before anyone had heard of coffee.
She was last seen slicing cucumbers, throwing ribbons out a window,
tapping out an old song with her moccasins, ruining the linoleum.

Full Moon

In tonight's grip
your confusion looks like clarity,
your window like a mouth,
your desk a sumptuous table
and the china cabinet like you might
crack it open for the first time since
your grandmother left it
to a cousin who didn't want it.
You remove the medieval service
and if the fifteen-pound carafe
is made of lead so what.
You could have anything on underneath
your gray-green pants, and this dinner
of leftover stew could be studded with berries
that will kill you before dawn.
You might not watch a DVD afterwards,
noncommittally searching out
your companion's hand,
edging towards her breasts.
You may throw her on the table, breaking it,
because it is an Ikea piece of shit.
You are not disposed to consider
whether this will harm her. You are
even less disposed to consider condoms.
Perhaps you will bathe in the snow afterwards
while the exhausted parents in the neighborhood
fail to try to arrest you to end your joy.
It is suddenly obvious that harm must be done
for anything to flourish—the perfect expanse of snow
has to be melted where you fall hot within it,
the table had to go, and the kid across the way
who is being raised, barely, on nectar and crackers
has to see you splinter your imaginary cage
with the mace of singing naked on the lawn.
You are making a happy little pervert of him,
and it is good. Too many years you spent
as a miserable pervert and no one ever
did a single thing to help.

Apologia for Lechers

When you see the topless teenage girls
sunbathing in Mallorca, their grins
traveling towards the corresponding
teenage boys, who run and chortle
in that casual way that's almost always an act,
you may say, good, let these young, lithe
beauties enjoy one another's perfect bodies
and empty hearts, let them not be squandered
on the lapping, desperate love of some
old slob or needy woman.

You realize that blond is not a color but the way
no part of them is made of earth. All dust in them
has come from stars with trembling half-lives
that sing softly, *there is no other moment.*
They are stupid as deer which saves them
from the ugliness of philosophy,
rip tides in the Balearic,
its botulistic trash, which saves them
from the mistakes that thinking causes.

Or then again you might scan those legs, those
chests that have their own assertions against man's
and nature's laws, chests no one can govern,
and you might observe that they don't know
how rare the girls they practice love on are.
And that boy who wets her lips
could be any other spearfishing from the jetty
for all she cares, because the world
is full of mirrors: sun gleam, water's surface,
a best friend's tinted glasses whose name
she won't remember the summer after next,
and that makes it easy to see nothing at all.

You may see that, like victims of thirst
or ignorance, they'll drink anything, take work
that amounts to slavery, buy lobster
from the factory store until their credit's gone.

When the knock comes at the door, they'll turn
to the middle of the bed where the disaster
of time will dawn in what last night was a lover.
They have never noticed anything before;
now everywhere they look the mirrors
distort tirelessly those sheer lines, those colors
that came in gaily from outer space
just to gad about a day and die,
that you and I saw on the beach, and pined.

By now you love them, want to save them
from the idiot in the bed, the coked-up
groupie in the bathroom. Why should they
never again make love to a slender boy
now they've discovered what one is?
If you could you would take one to Mallorca,
set a wide-brimmed hat upon her faded head,
turn her towards the jetty dripping gods
and say, *It's alright, my dear, go on.*
At the hotel you order *palo* and watch
peasants batter octopi against the rocks.

Part II

Light is used not for reading or writing or sewing but for dispelling the shadows in the farthest corners.

—Jun'ichirō Tanizaki

Elegy with Argentina

You had never lost anyone and wanted to see grief,
so we went to Plaza de Mayo where mothers marched
twenty-five years around the fountain, between stalls
selling flags and the cathedral, white as knuckles that fire
a gun for the first time. They shared their abundance with us
like bread beneath the palace where Evita lifted her hands,
and Juan Peron's body swallowed her collapse.

•

The Spanish empire was made and remade with silver ingots
and they chime in *Argentina* but not in the currency
paid for votes or changed to dollars on the blue market.
In Santa Rosa, we went to the end of a dock on the manmade lake
with a thermos and in the dark I imagined everything bigger,
more complex than it was, the middle class richer, each building
more sound, roses lavish. I began my apprenticeship
in waiting, but never learned to wait forever for the beloved,
for a set of teeth that could be identified, confirmed.

•

Two hours from Neuquén you see the Andes tower
at the end of the road your bus has broken down on,
teaching contrast, how the flag omits the clay desert,
the reddened pampas grasses, but preserves snow and sky.
With no distractions, nothing to mark time, the disappeared
scream whether you listen or not. We want to hoist
the white flag over our troubled lives, to give the desert back—
the mothers are albatrosses stranded in the doldrums.
They fold me into their ceaseless work.

Mentor

Argentina 1974 – 1983

Like every student I want you,
grateful to have been revised to taste.
Records did not prevent me from discovering
how you possessed me into absolution.
Someone remembers my arms when I wove
through the block party belly dancing.
Another says my hair was black, another auburn,
a third common brown. Many believe I had hair.
Someone remembers telling me a joke,
that I was judgmental and loud.
Part of my name's been restored.
No one appreciates your art more than
your backward Galatea, unobtrusive as air,
begging you silently to lavish again the white paint.
You are a son of the sun, and like the sun
lookers squint against your work, unable
to take in the extent of it, inarguable, unproofed.
Baptismal kerosene, honesty of daylight,
you raised me before your witnesses
lined against the cement wall, taking
and giving orders according to the diurnal pattern
you got from Saturn before you felled him
and fed his evidence to the ocean.
Ushuaia eres. Nothing can be south of you.

Grave

I or everyone dreamed it before
it was invented before our eyes
off the path we had walked so often.
I had looked for it and found briars or
a long clean-picked calf gleaming
accusation. Then a hollow within the trees
where a donkey stumbled in the rain
twisting its leg in legs. Like a child
to a breast, we felt out its meaning.

Stay of Execution

I trespass the hills of this valley
of microclimates and wild deer
where water bubbles unanswerable
from the middle of a field and a pond
is the secret name of privacy.
Everyone feels they've survived something,
not something predictable, patterned,
but unusual, intended
by some hand to kill them.

How, with all those different shapes,
do snowflakes lock together
to flatten the iridescent down
of spent milkweed to a gleamless mat
the melt leaves bare?

A farmer quarries stone by stone
and the next winter seems already to be laying down
its fat and ambition in Uruguay. A blackbird
sings her nerves, and she is right; her mate,
eggs, health cannot be counted on.
The plane which seems gentle aloft
has already ruined nests and the water
may not be drinkable next year.
Prey change season by season
with the weather that drives them
right or left or to death.
Nothing is as resilient as hay, thriving
on the blade.

Mule deer almost somersault, unnecessarily
fine and high, to another patch of leaves
and make a show of avoiding me. At nine months old
they are born in the sun that astonishes grass green,
casts shadows bigger than their fish. The deer are
keystones between everything they eat

and what eats them. Flies swarm
an impossibly slender foreleg
unexplained near a stream.

Biography of a Poet

Once you loved women often,
fiercely; you found them at night
with your hands.

Now you reread Quevedo
until you forget
carefully, gradually, everything

but Ava Gardner.
You practiced:
a car at the national library,

your only sheets at the laundromat,
Ivan's face over the child he killed.
Night lets the wrong sail out

and a spark lights up the room
before it shorts the electricity.
Once in streetlight

you smoothed a string tie against your chest.
Someone might say
that is where you were contained

if you were contained.
Jacarandas tear their dresses
and someone wearing glasses

records it as fall.
Then too soon the world
forgets you back.

Portrait of a Young Man

A man who has drowned no longer fears the water.
So let us call him drowned, and let us say
that in a very still lake his beauty was a stone
looking up from it, marbled, wet, inviolate.
Let us say I swam this lake when I was a lonely child,
and swam it later as a lonely woman, shivering,
feeling my breasts tighten in the cooler air.
For the sake of argument, I loved him, or rather
the light sometimes broke through the pines.

Palimpsest

Argentina 1978

Behind everything you see, my image is a stain
troubling this jacaranda, the tall sisters sipping beer
at a sidewalk table, confetti spilling from skyscrapers
after a Cup game against Africa or the Balkans.
To be cast beneath time and vellum, to serve a practical cause,
is something I understand from opposite the one-way mirror.
Your side is brightly lit, and sometimes that feels like privacy.
I am blind and invisible, both. Sometimes the illusion
is nearly reversed, and I think I see your face in the haggard man
holding a stethoscope to my chest to see if I have survived
this round, or because he thinks there is something,
he could not be certain, or swear in a court, underneath.

Perhaps

If I can be delicate as a fugue,
as an omelet, as a flute of champagne,
if I can tiptoe over rivers
where lovers have gone to drown,
if I can elude every drop of rain
as it rushes, if I weigh what breath
weighs, and weigh less, then perhaps
I can slip out of my country
as a thief would: deftly, undetected.
Differ only in my reasons.

Feast of the Assumption

Voiceless, you steal cherries
and rearrange the shelf of plays.
I have stopped answering silence
as a matter of principle. Tomorrow

everyone will make soup,
drenching the air with animal fat
and cries to the Virgin.
Luci has much to pray for—

her brother, her check, that the dead
and lost stay put. She stomps
her misery out on the ceiling,
cutting morcilla into oil, hurling

someone at the floor. She arrives
with an empty cup for sugar,
one nipple slipping from her robe.
Or she tries to sell a necklace

of teeth she found in the street.
Tomorrow she will march
through San Telmo
to the sagging music of tubas,

but my holy day of obligation
is always now. I cannot stop you
trespassing the onionskin walls;
you fail to stay in the teacup you poison,

the Kandinsky you distort.
You have forgotten to expect
my confession; I've forgotten
the location of Italy. What goes

in the hands you hold out?
I've tried coins and lye
and colleagues and love,
and nothing stays put.

Medea

I did not expect the day to end in dawn,
or the river in the photograph to flood
the living room. But I expected to see you
again: upright, studied. Wearing your summer

of meat in the Azores and pelagic freedom.
Instead you haunt Congreso,
crossing the stone bridge invisible where
a girl jumped from it thinking of her grandfather.

More than one ghost can play
your tortured Jesuit tune. In Paris
they sell themselves on straw mattresses,
buy brandy, live on regret

as the rich live on fashion.
The mice eat the feathers in their hair
when they lie under windows remembering sleep.
Holy candles burn a day and a half, lit with coins

needed for other things. The gods
feast on women's misery, paying out
promises. They rarely wake from their clouds
to take up lorgnettes

and tell the world what they were dreaming,
which someone will call writ, another
thunder. I recognize your voice in their nonsense,
sweeter than being young or right.

Disappeared

Argentina 1974 – 1983

In dream the truth was revealed:
how I began by combing your hair out
on the table
and lifting your temples from the bone,
relieved your head of your face.
I compromised what tied you
to the world, filled
your stomach with sand,
cleansed fingerprints, trimmed off
teeth. I brought you
into the untroubled sky
and unmade you in the bright air.
Violins rose to your vast freedom,
my one-time Communist, my whore
renewed. Angel scoured by current,
this is no Roman garden of justice.
I have not made an example of you.
See the sacrifice of the holy man:
free of identity, you wed
the ocean as equal, yet I
still tread the valley of work—
the souls that need erasing
never give me peace.

Videla in Prison

Civilization restored, his torture is the singing
of inmates for things like pussy that show they're fed.
The purposeless expectation of salute, of appeal
in the Marxist courts, notes from mistresses
he never let see him in the act of love, and who now
cannot be proven to have lived. How God decides
who lives to be old is God's affair. Videla knows
how he decided, and he knows that he lives on
in the country God abandoned in the Falklands. Yes,
Videla loves opera and hears it in his calm, clean mind.
The music is ordered and the stories always end
in purging death. Death we knew was coming
and leaned into languidly, gratefully, like Christ.

A Story about Departure

My dreams differed in their animals:
lion, deer, ghost. None pursued me,

indecipherable in moss. Awake,
I was night's cellmate, pacing and changing

the room where I thought. Mine was
an abundance of house, ditches

at last clear of purple vetch, its green hay,
when you arrived, a drink in your hand,

the woods at your back. I backed inside
but should have walked into the lake, asking,

How did you create the world we lived in?
Wine travels from vessel to vessel,

bad at spontaneity, unable to laugh back.
The actor I understudy is audible

within her dressing room, coughing.

Siddhartha

I could come back as
an egret lancing the marsh;
perhaps the osprey

once disappointed a good man.
And if human—
longer-legged, sun-colored?

I could need your beauty less
but earn it more—planting cosmos
in other people's yards,

giving my window box to milkweed.
I could find out where the twins in the sky
were born, why skin that's been hit turns blue.

You could be a canvasback
or a zinnia a gentle child loves
beyond other zinnias.

Or we are attached to this life
as a painting of oranges is nailed
to a wall in a forgotten hotel.

And it is no illusion
that you cannot be recovered
from any reliquary,

some path stiff and same as hell.

Theory of Relativity

Waking, you discover
our life lasted a few minutes;
only women in paintings live slower.

The truth of backs is
the towel will never dry them. The tsunami
gathers but does not land.

Even destruction
is beyond the gods who statue lush Tahiti.
Did you once think nights

only ended if you fell asleep?
If plums imagined
the basket that contains them,

then Sunday, then summer.
I walk correcting the meadow's tangles
and my fingers lose their order.

It is not in our power
to reverse the oversweetened coffee,
to become mistaken.

Part III

Let the high Muse chant loves Olympian:
We are but mortals, and must sing of men.

—Theocritus

Fractal Geometry

Looking for a place to stash a key on the porch, or a love note
you should not have anymore, or fifty thousand drug dollars
just for this week, you realize that all the places you think of
are the same you would think of if you were the one looking.
Why not look now, or now and then, for what might be hidden?
What is your lover, roommate, coworker, keeping almost
in plain sight? Perhaps it's duty to rid them of their secrets
and superfluous keys. We know from political rhetoric
that social programs only make people dependent on them.
Well Mrs. Jovovic next door should learn to remember
her damn fob when she leaves her apartment once a month.
Christmas accounts, too, must breed this sort of weakness.
You need to just not spend that money by being constantly aware
of abstract future expenses. I should empty your EpiPen
and like Jeff Bridges in *Fearless* you will eat tree nuts on a cliff.

It is dizzying imagining all the spaces things can fit into.
Where is a bank account? A password yields a number
but not the place or the look of the bills or any fact,
like whether a phone number is written on one, or whose.
The ocean can drive you crazy with its paranoiac concealments.
Manatees, coral reefs, krakens and mythic monsters
no one can prove aren't real, and the big guns: shipwrecks,
garbage, undersea islands of netted toothbrushes and razors
and the ten million gallons of oil that disappeared
in the Gulf of Mexico but must be there. You even heard
there is a lake underneath the sea, which has probably
already been misplaced or the map that located it tucked
thoughtlessly into a garment bag after an oceanographers' conference
and then donated to Goodwill because its left wheel broke.

Surely fish and algae, crabs and plankton live there, evolved
for nowhere else. And science tells us the smaller an organism
the greater numbers it can have because the less space each needs
to find purchase, so a crevasse that can support one orchid
can host a million duckweeds tucked into invisible notches.
Sometimes you want not just to enter that lake, but all its apertures.
Sometimes your thoughts drive you there, and you get trapped

behind an opening you somehow fit through when you entered.
Water within water finds its way into parts of you you'll never touch:
the inner ear, the nasal conchae, the ever so small pockets of your lungs.

Flowers Are Not Women

And women are not flowers
any more than a man
is a message nailed to a plinth
threatening challenge to strangers.
He is not always or ever an arrow
or leather unless you degrade him
with knife and spectacle.
A man is not a dog, or a woman a cat,
although all can be felled
by associations and cars and cold.
It is terrible how men can crumble
like pizzelles in a child's paw.
Or a woman harden as metal in a forge,
submit like a Camry to rust.

It is almost not enough to witness
the soft thing at the center, the delicate,
life-making thing, not humbled,
but caressed, grown large
and loved or just touched well.
It almost doesn't blot out jails
sick men enter to turn bad
or running men shot on lawns
like they stand for sport.

Men naked, men in love, men
imperiously ruled by the stone moon.
They are night-blooming things.
They cannot be made cheap
for sale in supermarkets
on Mother's Day or noncommittal
office birthdays. They can die without
interference though they rarely do.
They remind me of everything
I ever wanted to buy expensive dirt for
and water a little too often
and share with no one.

The Lover

Ah, the things you didn't choose—that tomato,
the green dress, some countries, one summer. It's a tease,
the perfect tilt of a hat the wind would never crumble
or a careless friend let dissolve in rain while he laughed at a parade.
Lady Chatterley is good, but *Women in Love*
would have surely been better—at the only game you didn't attend,
your nephew finally made a goal, and that concert
that sounded dull and far, Woodstock, you definitely should have gone to.
And what you did instead, the walk in the rain,
the quiet dinner under the dogwood,
was just plain stupid, you idiot. How could you
have cut your hair, long as Chile, that we all coveted?
Or—all the boys were after you until you grew
your hair out. It makes you look like a plant.
If you had had that birthmark removed when you
were eleven, as your mother suggested, you might
be married now, but the scar you hid under a glove
could have softened the man you chased, if he'd only seen it.
After all, he was the one you really loved, not these you've wasted
the years on, the one good bloom you get—see how it rises off your skin
like heat in a mirage and moves skyward—a stray balloon
tickling birds the color of persimmons.

Survivor

When the rain starts you are still
a quarter mile from home with a piece of bark
balancing decapitated violets against the breeze.
Do you like how a song is tethered to its start
like an addiction to drugs or being someone's daughter?

He left like a cloud with business
in the north Atlantic and you went
to the canvas he usually stands in front of with his life,
his few needs you magnify for the joy of meeting them.
For three days the sun
gives the excuse of watering the garden
to stop you making the pasta too early or
defrosting unnecessary steak. You learn
that you have forgotten to like new music
and how to dine alone, start fights to win.

You cut oregano and try to drown the dirt from it.
The answer to your question is that you hate
that the freedom in the middle doesn't last,
and you hate the freedom in the middle.
Music forgets but not the violinist.

Winter is the beginning and end of weather;
this is a rehearsal.

The Heaven of Poets

after Dickey

Your brother is not there. He's gone
to the Heaven of Athletes, starting on the lacrosse team
beside his son, the center. They are the same age.
His wife is with them, her balance outrageous,
beam routine performed in mid-air.
Her limbs reach unfathomably.

Your mother passes through occasionally
carrying rosemary; the peripheries of Heaven
are always troubled with mothers. There
is Virgil's mother, dressing olives.
Mrs. Berryman has picked up someone
at one of the many bars. They keep glancing
at their children, looking like saints.

There's a trout stream full of intelligent fish
who elude the hooks of those who love money.
Sometimes you find your father on shore,
taking a break with a coke and pretzels,
hypothesizing about the hatch. He has
a place here—still, this heaven is not for families.

Usually they sit at wrought iron outdoor tables
where no one pays for drinks.
Everyone orders bourbon; the waitresses
have forgotten how to spell anything else.
There are boisterous fights about Bowers
and accents grow stronger as the South is again
defended. No one in Heaven leaves Virginia.

Without sickness, the drunken poets stumble home
to tear at each other's bodies. The nights are longer
to accommodate their mischief. When they wake,
heads seizing, bodies tangled, they stand
under a shower that may run years, their love

no different than it was on Earth, but now
they have the time they always needed
and were never promised, to observe water
coursing over cherished skin, to name everything.

Elegy with Africa

All summer we waited for night to fall—
first drinking, then dinner, then the sweet release
from each other in sleep; in dreams we walked
circling lives we couldn't locate. Not until you left
did daylight relent, then night marooned me
between curtains, looking out.
You Barishnikoved through our dreamt-of theaters.
New York pulled storms into it and swept them away
before I felt I had them, and as they departed,
the sick half-light painted a clear, if bruised picture
of one of the views I had prayed for and been given.

•

They've given the richest continent to thieves
who water the unstoppable desert with blood.
Who court immortality in Lincolns, flirting
with gods that are never full on goats.
In hunger, the markets were strung up with monkeys
with pathetic faces and the lines for medicine
grew so long they became an independent occasion
for death. The sky watches and grows enamored
of the first good man she sees. She wishes for arms,
lest he not discover the new meaning of rain.

•

The apartment with too many bedrooms mocks
every emptiness you knew. With no one to waste money
on flowers, the tables grow infinite. Set a wine glass
here—later you will move it to the sink or carry it
upstairs. When the snow arrived, far from teasing
an early spring, it cut the ribbon of a fathomless winter
that originated in your body. The cold bled
through your feet into the tectonic plates, the ocean
swelled and a shudder crept up the spine of Japan.

You stand in a line you will never reach the front of,
your hand out, your legs buckling, wanting to recover less
than to receive the pardon that ends the nightmare
of sudden and gradual disappearance.

Phaeton

I was younger here once
seeing these spectral clouds that ride
the hills that make the valley.
You were someone else: a timid man
looking at me like I might invent snow
or animate the lightning-wrung elm.
We weren't even in love yet—
there was that much to go around.
I've drunk enough wine to look up:
the fireflies have abandoned
the abandoned field, the goldfinches
have taken their battles south.
The sun, like a teenager,
cannot set soon enough.

Love Poem for Malcolm X

I won't compare the color of your skin
to food or drink, accuse you of demagoguery,
say assalamu alaykum or make promises.
I make no references zoot suits or Armenians.
I reference sex and pan-Africanism
and the sublime. I circle disappointment
like an animal that doesn't understand. I arrive
without my dress on, tattooed from within.
I appear in your jail cell lame and sainted.

I made the mistake of believing in the world;
for a little while people found that beautiful.
The dreams I danced with, blond man, a place to live,
abandoned me for heretic.
I blame the world which wants our children,
our looks, which finds dazzling ways
to remind us we are small.
Which bought us terrible suits and sent us
to Harlem and away from Harlem.
Which will never admit its rotten heart.
You can talk about this in the laundry room
because it's self-evident.

I thought to change my mind
was an act of humility, proof I sought truth.
No one has believed in truth since Garvey.
I touch your socks where you sit on your eternal rug.
I listen to you without apology or revision.
I presume to point my finger
at the government of the United States,
to touch Africa and the American poor.
I go to the grave of Martin King and demand to know
why the geraniums are dry.

I lay down the sword after a long day in the desert,
a long thousand years in the desert.
Rolling up the entrance to the tent, I breathe in

roasting meat and cardamom coffee. I lose my head
and praise the world that lavishes suffering.
There you sit, finished with food, finished with blood.
Stricken and irreverent, I lean in toward your lips
and try not to curse the air for what it isn't.

To the Departing Beloved

1

The tulips have opened so wide—
they will never be more beautiful.
If I failed to show them to you
it was because I couldn't bear it.

2

I planted seeds a month ago
that are sprouting now.
Thai purple basil, parsley,
cilantro, your favorite,
oregano, chives.

3

This spring, remembering the last.
The lilac stings,
the white dogwood burns.

4

Birds are tender,
preening and playing.
Ceaselessly reviewing their affairs.
I've heard of a goose
that, seeing her mate killed,
gave up eating.

5

In our imagined wedding,
our friends clamor to object.
Then someone yells, "The lamb is done!"
and everyone lifts his wine.

6

Deserts unfolding over continents,
reefs blooming, branching, ossifying.
Trees wearing ice like sheer gloves—
the night you broke your silence
to alert me to the moon,
large as Texas.

7

Travel was the loneliness I chose;
at the opera,
in the midst of the aria,
profound silence.
That was before I met you.

8

I went to trouble with my looks:
dresses, bracelets, rouge—
it seemed like none of it mattered. Then,
none of it mattered.

9

No way to tell what things I loved for themselves
and what things I loved because of you.
If it were possible to sort it out,
I wouldn't.

Procession of Santa Lucia

In silver one week a year you loom
and abandon by Christmas
Sicily for your shuttered privacy.

No one is more wanted or
kept closed or rudely opened
than you are in a death

preserved by Italians amazed
at chastity, lesser miracles.
The dagger

never leaves your neck,
and no golden curls
catch fire.

Your brocade screen
prevents the spectacle
of further sainthood: no one sees

the salt tears or blood
that prove
the infinity of your affront.

You tug against
the orders of men and their courts:
virginity—marriage—brothel—sepulcher—

closet—bier and the heaving
of twenty bodies under your weight.
A thousand candles light

in paper cups, and cripples walk
the whole six hours
leaning on barefoot mothers.

Fuji

There's no end to how you ruined everyone's life,
dithering, alighting into every breeze like a seedpod,
trying to be taken, to get drunk and forget yourself.
Whatever you gave was something already owed,
but what you took, prepared to suffer but not
the right way, was tallied joyously by a spinster
who never had the benefit of your chances. Tallied
by men who, wronged by your love, still emerged
dapper, shining, with girls smiling so big at them
they could tie a tie in the reflection off their teeth.
They've forgotten the eloquent, tragic curses they levied
against the words you sent, as no one does, on paper.
No one says that the promises of lovers are beautiful
not because they will be kept, but as mountains are beautiful
with or without coal or timber or ravenous, invisible gods.

Katabasis

Because it was a dogwood we sat under, or because
someone wrote this out like a coda, or because of nothing,
because there are no causes, I fell into you and came out
of a French river whose name sounded like a cello sounds
when the cellist is neither practicing nor performing.
How long can I follow these banks, startling mallards,
slicing my feet on wine bottles? I will take this walk
all the way to the Mediterranean through strawberry festivals,
through fields of irises, through abandoned train routes,
catching flying neckties and pastries that careless people toss.
I will drown until I arrive where I left you, right hand
on a dogwood branch, on your lips a thousand thousand ways
to say brunette more beautifully.

You Are in Ukraine

In Argentina we fooled two weeks of January
splashing in the cold wine sold
in unmarked bottles on Plaza Dorrego
and talked to street tango dancers
about the past but not the future.
She says she will probably never
get another visa to Europe and looks
over me at you longingly.

There are not many churches;
there are many plaques showing
where people were seized from their apartments,
some of them steps from the cathedral
where someone who is now Pope prayed
against the baying response of the ambivalent.

If you know what to look for, there is almost more missing
in Argentina than what is there,
rich with ghosts no matter the peso's value.
I am just one of the slender ranks.

There I wander alone down Santa Fe.
There I stare at the Andes. Things in the past
seem far away, but I touch them
as we move through life carrying what we share
that makes it tolerable.

Few are the saints
who can bear this silhouetted suffering.
Your absence casts me back
to my place in the procession.
The summer solstice is Sunday;
but there is no moment long enough
for each of us to recite our names.

Elegy with the Soviet Union

You dreamed you loved a woman and then dreamed her
onto a train bound for Stalingrad. Strangers called out
to your black car from the streets wanting your confession
or your advice on buying fruit. You said, *they talk this way*
in the Ural mountains and I've never learned another.
There was no electric light and you invented vodka
with nothing but your mouth and thirst. You changed
from widower to soldier; you became consumed.

•

You smolder atop the inadequate cool of ice
and pickled mushrooms—eating caviar to kill
the ocean-hating demons. Sturgeon swim upstream
and you take the train to Bryansk, rocking in fevered sleep,
ordering tea in glass tumblers set in filigree, searching
the visible forest for dachas, proof of one of winter's names—
you hear hoarse-voiced angels, cats crazed with sadism.
In memory departure and return are simultaneous.
Time undresses, fever passes, dreams feast on your mind.

•

Illiterate angels cloud the church with their quarrels,
weighing down the overgrown beards—you've witnessed a tall woman
doubled under the polished boot of her husband, her razor
cheekbones smothered in leaves. You believe the myth that stone
chills the womb explains the missing generation,
the living bewildered by matching streets, hallways,
bedrooms of The Party's deliberate repetitions—get off the train
and into any bed; the woman in it will take you for her lover.
When you touch her she will wake, ask if this is, then, a man.

Kingfisher

Salt and fresh water meeting
in the estuary, fiddler crabs
touched everywhere by both.
Braving deer ticks to gather cattails
for the craft show
where I sat in a little chair beside my father.

•

A piece of scrap wood crenulated
and polished by long drifting—
my father takes it to mount a kingfisher
he has stained
and left drying in the sun.

•

The universe will never give up
piecing atoms into jetties, marshes,
creeks and sand sharks.
Some summers invisible algae redden the sea.

•

A tropical storm moves towards the coast—
even before it's given a woman's name,
baymen feel the clams sink deeper.

•

Merganser lake-serene, puffin fluffed in wind.
Black swan dressed for the Vatican,
stilt poised to spear a fish.
My father's workshop
teems with heavens.

•

Some things cannot be understood
or overvalued.
The first is the love of fathers.

Every Day You Are the Oldest
You've Ever Been

A magnificent sky stretches over the New Jersey Turnpike,
in the firm middle between sun and rain, as the season
is neither summer nor fall and the heart is not sure
whether it is any longer young enough to fall in love or what
lies beyond the storm the demoiselles crest this flight north.
Even something as simple as the cold will not stay still
to be grasped, and the man I loved, his pure smile at an odd thing,
his gait in morning, has gone somewhere there is no telephone.
The book of butterflies gets heavier in the threadbare satchel
that belonged to every grandmother's grandmother.
The attic bursts with everything that's ever been forgotten,
preserved by heat and the indifference of nesting squirrels.

Who shall I thank for the things not yet bruised by disaster?
My mother is alive, the river, somewhere, is full of fish
that are difficult to catch. Some cats are loved.
When my grandmother moved out of her last house, I took
the high school portrait of my mother and two early swans
my father made. Now, groaning in a hospital, she has let go
of things rich and cheap, quiet and loud, and twists
through the last days of her life trying to get comfortable
against a rotting leg. Standing outside, everything seems
too beautiful to be the only god, and so deaf, even acts
go silent. I want to tell you I never wished to keep the world
to myself, that once I drove beside my grandmother
in the early morning before the sun was up and found
even Florida electric and mysterious, that I am still that girl,
that if you can wait, I can be there tonight in time for dinner.

Notes

Part II

The Dirty War in Argentina lasted from 1974 to 1983, beginning during the presidency of Isabel Perón, consolidated by the 1976 military coup and ensuing regime led by General Jorge Videla, and ending when the military was forced to hold elections after its disastrous invasion of the Falkland Islands in 1982. The Dirty War was an official program (called the National Reorganization Process) by the military government against all Argentines it classified as terrorist or subversive. The first groups to be targeted were left-wing activists and militants, but the circle of those under suspicion grew rapidly to include students, journalists, psychiatrists, friends and family members of activists, and in the end no one in Argentina was safe from state-sponsored terrorism. The term "disappeared," or *desaparecido*, was coined to describe the status of Dirty War victims who were usually kidnapped and then either killed or imprisoned and tortured, but in the vast majority of cases never heard from again or discovered. The military government went to great lengths to conceal the whereabouts and outcomes of their victims and still continue in some cases to deny the nature of these crimes, which were justified and tolerated by the world community as fighting the Communist threat. The generally accepted estimate of disappeared Argentines is at least 20,000.

Part III

"Procession of Santa Lucia" refers to a celebration of the martyrdom of Saint Lucy (Santa Lucia) of Siracusa, Sicily. She lived briefly at the end of the third century, and, according to her story, wished to remain a virgin and distribute her dowry to the poor. Her mother arranged a marriage anyway, but after a change of heart helped her disperse her fortune. Lucy's betrothed appealed to the governor, who ultimately sentenced her to be defiled in a brothel. When no number of men or teams of oxen could move her from prayer to fulfill her punishment, they killed her. A 90-kilogram silver icon of her is kept covered in the cathedral in Siracusa. Every year on December 13 the icon is removed, carried in a massive, many-hour procession throughout the city, and left on display for a week until it is returned. The icon bears a dagger in the neck.